R. E. P. E. A. T.

resolve. edify. pursue. evolve. amplify. teach.

R. E. P. E. A. T.

resolve. edify. pursue. evolve. amplify. teach.

ISBN: 9798883356321

Wanna Share?!?

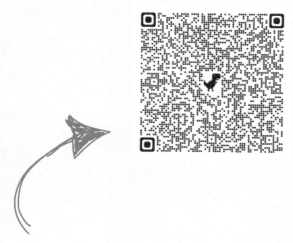

R. E. P. E. A. T.
resolve. edify. pursue. evolve. amplify. teach.

For every man, woman, and child, especially the youth.

Note: The pages in this book are centered purposely to remind you to stay centered. R. E. P. E. A. T. as needed

R. E. P. E. A. T.

resolve. edify. pursue. evolve. amplify. teach.

That's it love, you've done it. You've made it through the most challenging part, you've opened the book. Here's to the start of a serious but much-needed journey in the right direction that will propel you to the greater part of you.

Before we start at this very moment, take some time and grab a paper or notebook (whatever you have). The first step to resolving things in our lives is to start at the beginning. So, write down everything you remember from your beginning, good or bad; go as far back as possible. Start at the very beginning, your timeline of events, and be honest with yourself; no one else has to ever see your truth; your start. Draw a line down the center of your page like a vine; you can do it year by year like I did or just what you remember. Now, it is essential not to skip this. After you've done this, just put that paper or notebook away. Put it somewhere it can only be seen once it's time, but remember where you put it. Make a promise to avoid cheating yourself that you will only read it once you reach the end of this book.

Now, let us begin. My prayer is that you gain all there is for you to obtain and retain in this book and that your heart be open to receive it!

Chapter 1
Let's Get Covered

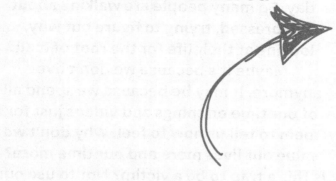

R. E. P. E. A. T.
resolve. edify. pursue. evolve. amplify. teach.

Lets's Get Covered
Resolve

Are we addicted to being entertained? In short, yes. We crave more and more every day. So many people are walking about depressed, trying to figure out why, looking at their life for the root of it all. Maybe it's because we don't live anymore. It may be because we spend all of our time on things and videos just for them to tell us how to feel. Why don't we value our lives more and our time more? Is this a trap to be a victim? Not to use our brains and resolve things with real solutions for some of these overly thought problems? Some would say yes; this generation and some that have come before them get caught up in things like money and people. The times have changed. Yet the people before us were the innovators way back when they had less to work with. Now that we have more to work with, there are no more innovators. Not one to start a trend in the right direction in life. Could this be because we don't know how to communicate or how we feel? We are losing our sense of self, but getting it back is not as difficult as one may think. It can sometimes just be hard to maintain. We need to start at the beginning to find the root source. Ask yourself what gives you peace and coverage in your life?

R. E. P. E. A. T.
resolve. edify. pursue. evolve. amplify. teach.

Lets's Get Covered
Resolve

What things in life make you feel comfortable and protected? I don't know about you, but it's the feeling of a warm blanket as I sleep, no matter the season. It makes me feel protected to have something covering me while I sleep; otherwise, I feel vulnerable and open. Some people can sleep anywhere and don't need that protection. A blanket isn't meant to protect us in actuality just to cover us; it's a material object that only gives us temporary warmth. When you think about it, we cover our physical items like our bodies, cars, houses, and even our devices. Yet, we just refuse to cover ourselves where it matters most. What about the coverage we need for our lives? The blanket that doesn't just cover our outer being but covers us completely inside and out. Why leave ourselves open and vulnerable to anything, letting the devil in to win? It's deeper than we think; it is beyond the emotional side of us. Leaving ourselves open can bring harmful things that take root and shape us into someone else. Why let the enemy who hates you and cares nothing about you in? Why aren't we protected? When people ask why God allows this or that to happen, I think, are you under protection? Do you know him?

R. E. P. E. A. T.
resolve. edify. pursue. evolve. amplify. teach.

Lets's Get Covered
Resolve

Have you ever prayed? Did you give your sinful life back to him to come under the covenant of Jesus? This is the world that we live in, not heaven. There is chaos and evil all about. We need to arm ourselves correctly for our environment. When you are outside and look around on a clear day, it's not actually "clear." There are things just floating all around that we'd only be able to see with a microscope. So when I say unclean spirits are lurking among us, we can not see it's real. Think about it; we can't see allergies, but in a certain season, they may affect you. To be protected from them, we need the right coverage from the ones who can see. Our Holy Spirit has a microscope to see where we can not. To be protected under the covenant from God, we have to be under his cover. It's Spirit against flesh against Spirit, fighting against realms of things that we can not see. When there is a covenant with God, then our Holy Spirit can guide us from things to protect us. What would that look like? To be covered under the most high God of all creation? To not worry, to not have pain that we couldn't handle anyway, not to have to fight certain battles that were never meant to be fought by us. Do you know what that would look like?

R. E. P. E. A. T.
resolve. edify. pursue. evolve. amplify. teach.

Lets's Get Covered
Resolve

Peace. Inner and outer peace. The greatest peace you've ever had! For me, I need full coverage; I might get the liability to save a bit of money on something perishable, but this is for my soul, so Lord, cover me fully! It makes no sense to not cover your eternity when this life is only temporary, like the blanket. I'm not here to force-feed God on anyone. I'm just going to give you the truth to light the two paths for you. Having eternal life with God is the inheritance that we all have the opportunity to have, but the choice to do so is up to us. We all have the choice to choose and know that with choice come consequences, like not having auto insurance and getting into an accident without coverage. Everything is a choice. Even if it's a law, we can choose to abide by it or not. Don't get what I'm saying wrong. We are loved by God and are all worthy of his love no matter the past if we're willing. If you are willing, then hopefully, this will be a way to help you choose. To be covered by God and utilize your coverage when needed or not to be covered and pay a hefty price, but first things first. Let's talk about the past before the present.

R. E. P. E. A. T.

resolve. edify. pursue. evolve. amplify. teach.

Chapter 2
Marry Your Path, Not Your Past

R. E. P. E. A. T.
resolve. edify. pursue. evolve. amplify. teach.

Marry Your Path, Not Your Past
Resolve

To start the process of living differently, we have to first resolve the things we've allowed in our past. Whenever you want to know the who, what, when, and why, we always have to start at the beginning. Unfortunately, going through the past is the beginning of that. Even though the past is in the past, we are surrounded so much by it, and it binds us and keeps us there as long as we allow it to. If we are bound to it, we will never move forward. Going forward means a new beginning. Like a new clock or a new day. When you lose a game, it's not over as long as you can replay it; just play again. You get a new clock and a new opportunity. I've watched my children not give up on a game until they've won. Looking at every time with a new outlook. Like, I can do this, not thinking at all about the loss. We should be more childlike in this area and start a new clock on a new day.

Stop just replaying the last days, months, or years in your new day. You have a new day. You can make new decisions on this day that can make better the things of yesterday. If we do this every day, eventually, the past will no longer bind us because we'll look at each day with a new set of eyes.

Most of us get this opportunity every day, and we take it for granted. We're not even promised a new day, and yet we go to bed at night expecting it. We go to bed with anger, discontent, and unforgiveness, not thinking it could be our last. No more new clocks or a new day to get it right. Just out of time. What good did that anger do to go to bed with or have that unforgiveness in our hearts? What was the gain? This doesn't change your life, outcome, or your circumstance. I think that we would get better every time and every day. I would think that we would progress like the things around us that we see every day. What would that look like? Eventually, we'd win, right? Why are we so determined to sabotage or make life harder? What a waste of time. Why not put that energy where it counts? Wouldn't that be ideal? That would help our lives to move us forward, evolving our current lives and life after us. What if we had to choose a path; what if our life depended on it? Well, it does. We take this opportunity that we get every day for granted without a thought. I once watched a movie where you had to play a video game for your life, and people would die if they lost.

This is that game, or more like a maze game. If you play it correctly and in the right direction, you reach home. If you play it wrongly in the opposite direction, then you will reach a dead end. You can not go back or just replay this game, though; you have to deal with the fact that your choices along the way landed you in a bad place, a dead end, or your end. Along this journey, there may be things that you can pick up to aid you in going a certain way, but there are always two choices. Things you know that only give you temporary life pleasures that lead you down the wrong path. Or the other choice of things that don't give you that temporary feel-good feeling but always give you everything you need to survive till you reach home. This is a life-or-death situation; it's not a game; it's real life, and there are two real choices. Long life with the Spirit of the Lord, or a long, slow, everlasting death. Don't take this everyday new life new clock for granted. We need to seek out the things along our paths that will aid us in getting home. We should not ignore the clues and confirmations or what they're trying to tell us.

One day, I was having a conversation about navigating life and how hard it can be to make better decisions from our past regrets. I tried my best to convey my words in a way that they could understand, but the words just didn't come out right. I needed them to know these things, but I couldn't put the words together. As I was trying to get it together, the Holy Spirit took over heavily, and my Spirit spoke these words. "You have to be humble enough to give and be given to, smart enough to play this game called life but not to get sucked in, strong enough to endure the pain but not let it consume you, wise enough to lead and not be aimlessly led, loving enough to love all and teach all despite everything, and Spirit ready to leave it all behind." In our past, there were good memories and bad memories, but we don't have to live our present time from our past time. We have the choice to move forward and start a new day with new thoughts and an openness for growth from yesterday. The best thing for us is to get on the right path that reaches back to a place that will be familiar and will give us comfort and peace: home.

The time to do this is now because the present time is all that we know we have, so we need not waste it. Wasting time in the past instead of using it to reflect on and gain knowledge is a waste of precious time from God. There have been bad, unforgettable things that happened in all our lives, either to us or to someone we know. I know firsthand that the past hurts, but if we don't take ourselves from it and look at it for what it was, then we'll be bound to it, and it will hinder our present and future. For example, there have been people in this world who have given up on life from hurts of their own and have gotten you or someone else caught in their pain. The pain from that hurt some of us to our core to be violated in whatever way it may have been. This could've been something big or small, but if we feel pain from it, then it's real. The thing about hurt is that we have to know that when hurt is involved, there is a beginning to it. The beginning of that pain from their hurt led this person to anger that took root in them, and they never healed from it.

It festers and most times if no one helped them through it, it's because they were also not equipped with the tools needed to heal so it falls on to the next. It's a domino effect. God says that we perish from lack of knowledge, not knowing destroys us all. This is why living and dwelling on our past hurts or regrets is a waste of time. The people or things have since moved on to face their hurt and the people they've hurt in some way. So, while we sit and let the past run into our future we only bring all that baggage that came from it with us. Being that we're not in that time of hurt we need to have a way of letting it go. When Jesus was on the cross and he was about to cross over he said "Father why have you forsaken me". There have been so many testimonies of people who say that your life flashes before you as you pass. I think that because Jesus was a sacrifice for our sins he asked this of God because he had to see all the hurt and pain that we were going to endure and it was so much to bear. It's not that Jesus couldn't handle it but to just see it was a lot because we couldn't ever bear all the sins of man.

Just think of all the things that we've heard or read about. Jesus already took on the pain that we hold onto. I don't want to be a part of the ones that make that suffering somehow in vain. I don't want to let that great act of love be taken so lightly by not fully letting go, not living in my past but instead living in the present and future for God. Let us stop holding on to things that we have no strength for. If you're ready to lay it all down at the feet of Jesus, then simply just do so. Tell our Father all of what keeps you bound even in your present time. Release it all to him and, like a baby, cry on the shoulder of God because he can bear it all. Allow the love of God to give you peace from it and be healed. If you're ready to move on, you can; all you have to do is let it go. It can be a task, but the freedom you will feel from the peace you release will be a lot easier to carry. We have the keys to unlock the chains of our past by praying to God for a release from it. Do it now because now is all we are promised; don't let another day pass when you could be free to start anew. If you've taken time to do this, Amen; now we can go into the edification process.

We need to work out muscles that we never used before. We need to start with the questions about God's purpose for us here. Let the edifying begin.

Chapter 3
Why Do We Need To Know Everything?!?

I have always been the type to ask questions. Someone told me that there are no stupid questions when you don't know, so I'm not shy about this. When I was a girl, I had elders trying to guide me down the better path of life. I asked a question that I never could get the answer to till I was older. I'm sure most of us have asked this or thought about the question of why. If we came from heaven, why do we need to come here and live on this earth? What's the purpose? The simple answer is to get back home, but what's the explanation? So, here's the real behind the reason from the understanding I've gotten. The heavens were created before the earth. How long the heaven was before God created the earth is not known. However, when you read the word from the Bible, the devil, who was once an angel, was cast from heaven at some point by God. This is something that took place, I believe, before the earth was even finished. When Adam was created in the Garden of Eden, God didn't just create the garden with one tree. God created many trees in the garden, but only two of the many were important. One tree was the tree of life, and the other was the tree of knowledge of good and evil.

God told Adam that he could take and eat from the forest but not from the Tree of Knowledge of good and evil. From the beginning, God gave us the mercy of choice. When I first read this, it didn't hit me because I already knew that God had given us the choice of serving him or the devil based on our daily decisions. Then, just like before, I wondered why we got the choice to choose in the first place. The devil was sent out of heaven with no real timeline of when, but when the devil was cast out, he was cast out along with his angels who shared his beliefs. God says that we are born in sin and part of that sin comes from the sin of the devil. The first to sin against our creator. This sin caused a rift and caused the devil to be cast out, along with the angels who shared his beliefs. God, being the father he is, sends us to earth also to make a choice. So we can choose to go back home to heaven even after seeing what the devil has to offer or stay here on earth with the devil just deeper down into it.

God has given us things on this earth
so that we don't doubt his existence.
The first thing God gave us was the
Holy Spirit to guide us and the soul
that's connected to the Holy Spirit to
be the balance that keeps us together
between our soul and body. I'll talk
more later about this Trio, but their
functions are very important. The
second one is the only begotten son
of Our Lord God, Jesus
(Yahuah/Yahusha), who was given to
show us in the form of man the way
and truth of God's word. To be a living
example of what to follow, we needed
to be led by a visual example. The last
is what Jesus left behind for his
disciples to testify: the Bible. The
written book of what we need to
reference from things that don't
change with time. Solomon said,
"There is nothing new under the sun."
This reference was about the life on
earth we live. Anything that we're
going through now, there is a
reference of help to it in the Bible. Our
father set forth these things so that
we wouldn't have questions. So that
we could have a guide here with us to
make a sound choice for our final
destination.

I don't pretend to know everything about God. God says that we weren't meant to know everything. If we did, it would leave no room for openness to grow or to be childlike. For me, it's a benefit not to know it all. The things that I do know, I share out of obedience and love. When my Spirit moves, I move, listen, and wait to be instructed. When I'm being told to do something or say something, I'm very vocal. There is a lot we don't know, but if we continue to keep ourselves humble, we will always be available and open to growth. Sometimes, when we think we know it all, things become too complex and full of confusion. We can complicate things by overanalyzing and falling through traps. Some things in life just weren't meant to be so difficult, like God. We're so busy looking into God's past, Jesus's past, looking to fact-check or get the identity confirmation right. It's something that we've all done not to feel or look stupid, but in hindsight, it's just for ourselves. God wants us to just focus on him and deal with our hearts. There are just some things we won't ever know or answers that we'll never get. Holding on to them and pondering over the "facts" will just keep us stuck in a rut.

It's like, what's the reason for it? To just know? What will it change? Now we can say we know; then what? Will this give us the gratification needed in life? We spend time in this new era of technology every day just gaining senseless knowledge. What has it changed in our lives to just know? We go every day not knowing whether it'll be our last, but that has never stopped us from dreaming about the future or making plans for the weekend. We just live in whatever way we see fit. Why does knowing the "truth" how, what, when, and where alter everything that surrounds us that will stay the same no matter what? Ask yourself, if you knew the answers, what would it change? Honestly? Cause if someone said oh well, you know God isn't real, and it was made up to keep you under control. What would that change? What has it changed knowing all of what we've heard about the world we live in? If your life was filled with joy, peace, love, family, and grace to live long and prosper. If you never had to worry, look over your shoulder, or burden your mind and body with heavy loads. What would it really cost you?

What does this carefree life gain you when you think about it? Does it come with peace and love, not having to search anymore, or chaos and more questions? It's a never-ending battle and a waste of precious time. Then, someone else would give you all these proof facts and scenarios of how that's not the truth to make you second guess it again soon after you're right back to square one. Do you get the redundancy? We do this to have more life control, yet we're still under control, knowingly. We have to answer to the higher authority for wasting this precious time. Not one person on the planet has no one to answer to, not one. If we search within our Spirit by spending time with God, that's one answer where we WILL find actual truth because the Spirit of truth lives within us! In turn, comes your peace and that blanket of protection you read about. With joy, love, and long life to be able to complete the mission of our purpose. I'd rather have a life of beauty; how about you?

Chapter 4
God Is Of Balance

R. E. P. E. A. T.
resolve. edify. pursue. evolve. amplify. teach.

God Is Of Balance
Edify

The body that we are born with is the only body that we'll ever get in this life. Our bodies are meant to last into the elder years, along with all their functions, so we are meant to take care of them. If we worked all day and didn't take a break to eat or sleep, what would happen? For me, it wouldn't last; I'd have to eat or get a nap or something. Our body will just shut down if it doesn't get what it needs to function. Most things that have balance need to start on a steady foundation. Too much of anything take us out of balance. For example, if there is too much exercise but not enough sleep, too much love without enough giving, too much food, and not enough water to wash it down,

You know, a scale will be unevenly balanced if you don't even it out, and so will we. We need an equal ratio balance so that we can stay centered. We can see how balance is a big part of life just by looking at the creations of God that are all around us. I urge you just to take a day and go to a park to spend the day just analyzing the world around us that God has made. Look out at the sky if you can't make it to the park or at the birds that fly by.

Pay close attention to the structure of balance that God has made. Trees could be older than us, but they have a strong, structured balance between the trunk and limbs. The trunk of a tree may have branches that branch out from all sides, but we will never see a thin trunk holding broad branches. There would be no balance to hold it upright without falling over. A bird that has one wing couldn't fly without the balance of two. For everything that God has created, there is an innate purpose to keep balance and order so the things around us flow like a river. We, as people, the creations of God, also need that balance. We can not fully function correctly without balance and order in our bodies and lives. Some of us have been off balance for a long while and have adapted to the dysfunction but wonder why there is no peace. Peace of self and peace of life around us only come from a strong structured foundation to create the balance that's needed. We would never pay all our bills but leave out the one that shelters us, right; that would be silly.

We need this balance. We have to stop making excuses for our imbalance and do the things necessary to structure our lives properly. There are three things that we'll get into in a moment, but first, we'll speak about our bodies. Our minds structure our bodies, so the health of our minds needs to be balanced for our bodies to function correctly. For example, if we are hurt by something or someone, we experience all the emotions that come with that hurt. If that hurt consumes our mind to where we are always thinking of it day in and day out, then it starts to create an imbalance in the body, and this is how depression starts. That depression will cause us not to eat or eat too much, but either one can cause a health issue. We need to eat for our bodies to function, but for our organs to function properly, we need not to eat as much. If we dealt with the hurt first off when it happened, maybe we would have gotten the balance that we needed to process the hurt mentally, and in turn, it wouldn't keep us from eating or make us overeat. The structure has to be there from the foundation, and the foundation of a healthy body is first the mind.

The peace that God gives to us from the love that he creates in us will give our minds that healthy foundation needed for our bodies. We don't have to sit and toil over things in our minds; we don't need to worry about tomorrow, no matter the reason. We need peace of mind and peace in our minds for the balance of structure, and God gives us that. We need to eat less and think more. Even when I type that, it doesn't seem right because I like to eat. When I say this, though, I mean that we need to consume less. For real, I could sit and eat an entire bag of chips, not the small bag, the big one, or a whole pizza. This is not the balance that our bodies need to function. Some things that we eat will make us sick if we eat too much of it. Try eating grease every day for a month, and you'll be sick, right? What's horrible is the grease from some of the food we eat. If we eat too much of it, we will have nearly eaten a month's worth of grease anyway. We have to balance what we eat to function our bodies, and sometimes, it's good not to eat at all. When I say not at all, I mean to fast our bodies.

Jesus did this in the Bible, and it's a great thing sometimes for the body to do for balance as well. I know it sounds backward not to eat food, but we're not talking about doing it forever. When you look at the structure of the body, you will see how hard it works to function. All that we do to it, from eating certain things, just adds to the work. Not eating sometimes gives the body a much-needed rest. God says to fast. I'm sure the creator of our bodies knows what they need. When you can, just go and pick up a book about the body and how it works or read it on the net; you'll be amazed. Believe it or not, our bodies also need a physical balance on the outside as well. People who say they don't like touch need more healing of the heart because the right hug can change our entire mood. God has designed our bodies to give off certain things like oxytocin that delight our bodies just from physical touch. No, I'm not saying to go out and just let people touch your body or just kiss strangers. Remember that God is of order; these things should be done in the ways that God intended them.

If you are in the balance of God (his covenant), you'll be more protective of your body and view it with respect. A kiss from your wife or husband, a hug from family or a friend, and even the cuddles of a fur baby are good for the body's balance. We shouldn't go a day without this, so if you haven't had it today, take your arms, wrap them around you as best you can, and hug yourself. Love is another big key to a healthy body, but there must also be a balance between them. So, let's do better with the health of our bodies in all ways so that we can have the order and balance to keep us upright. God says to love him with all our minds, hearts, and souls and to love each other also as well as ourselves. Love is the first commandment; that's just how important love is.

Chapter 5
Love Is Love & It Conquers All

There are so many descriptive things around us if we just look with a different mindset. As I was riding one day, I saw a young couple sitting on a curb next to an ice cream shop. I promise you I can not make this up. Now, notice I said I was riding and not driving, so I caught a nice glimpse of what was going on. He and she were smiling and laughing; he said something funny, no doubt because just from her smile, you could tell that she was all in, and so was he. Before I write this, I want to say that I'm a hopeless romantic. I loved to be in love; it's blinding, it's blissful, and it's exhilarating. It's a lie. I know you weren't ready for that last part, but it's just not the reality of what actuality is. We sometimes fall into love instead of just allowing love. When we first get into a relationship, we love almost everything about them. Even the small flaws we see, we're able to overlook when in love. From the woman's side, if you're not too picky, you will help him accomplish goals that you hadn't even accomplished for yourself. From the man's side, she's "sweetheart" or "baby girl" and can do no wrong. Even that little attitude of jealousy you think is cute, and you overlook all the emotions that detail who she is.

We will see something so broken and believe that our love will fix it. People are not perfect, and we will always do something to disappoint someone. This "in love" contract suddenly changes, and something clicks in you, and you wonder how you fell for this person in the first place. The more you were around them, the more you had to deal with real issues that caused sudden problems that you had never seen before. Whether it was something they did or said or didn't say, something made you start to doubt your love. Then the fights start, the hurtful arguments, and depending on how well they know you, it can cut deep, and now we are hurt, wounded. Both of you fight because you seek to be heard, thinking that the person you felt so much for will, in some way, have the capacity to understand even though they couldn't do so when they initially hurt you. Then the breakup makeup just to do it all over again thing happens, and you just hurt each other more. After all this, you find yourself too deep either by baby or years of life, so you stay in it. You endure even if it's starting to change who you are, hopeful that the feeling of being "in love" will just come back.

This "relationship" turns into just a ship with relations, and things fade to do I love them at all. Your "love" was conditional; so was theirs. It was blissful and exhilarating to be in love but blinding to the truth. Being "in love" is just an emotion, not reality; it wasn't real. Well, emotionally, it was real, but emotions fade like happiness, and it can be countered by time. If you've never felt the emotion of love, you will; we all do. For the ones who have, like me, it's ok to let the pain of that go to love again, but in the right way. There is a resolution of healing from the mindset and lies that we've been persuaded to believe. Simply wait for your Father to send the right person. Can we be in love and then choose to love that person even after the thing of being in love fades? Yes, but only because we chose to. We have to ask ourselves, though, are they under the covenant of God? Can they love us the way God says to? Are they doing this now, or will they in the future? I know I crushed some people with all that, but let me explain it further. Don't take this the wrong way; love can and should be a beautiful thing.

However, as of late, the word love and its true meaning have been diluted more and more. Like a currency can lose its value and become less effective, the word love has lost its effectiveness in having the power behind it that it was meant to. We really will break out the word love for food or material items just as quickly as someone that we're close to, like a family member or our child. That's a different kind of love, though, right? We don't love our food or material things like we love our parents or family. Right? Well, why not? Is love love? If you were to look in the dictionary, you would find multiple definitions next to the word love, even the dictionary has adapted. Understand that love is a vast word, but the real love of God is different. So when you say I love something or I love you to someone, it doesn't change the meaning or effectiveness of the true word because of your intent behind it. I would never put my car or food over my family, would you? Ok, so love should be in a better position based on how we use it because the definition of love in the dictionary (to sum it up) means deep affection. The word deep means extending far down, extreme.

When we say things like I love ice cream, we wouldn't go as far as to say I have a deep, intense affection for ice cream. Yet we would say this about a family member that we're deeply close to. So, the word love and its meaning is so intense that we should never use it to describe things that have only a momentary value to us. This is why being "in love" is just a concept; it's a momentary feeling. Why do you think it starts at the beginning of a love story? You meet, and you fall hard. Bam! You are in love. When you're in love, the state of being in love is so deep for us because of the physical effects of being in love; then bam, you're out of love like you read before. The true meaning of love wasn't meant to fall in or out temporarily. It was meant to be deliberate because true love is a choice. We choose to love because true love is unconditional. There is no true love that has conditions. I love you, but if you do this, oh, well, I used to love you; I used to be in love with you. That's love with conditions, which is not true love. True love is when you love someone, no matter the conditions. When they disappoint you, hurt you, and don't fit into your perfect mold, you still love them.

R. E. P. E. A. T.
resolve. edify. pursue. evolve. amplify. teach.

Love Is Love, & It Conquers All
Pursue

When you've loved someone past their flaws, that's true love. The actual words in love don't even go together; they're not one word; they're two, but we say them as though they're one. Only when I became more mature did I understand this about love being a choice and not a construct. We need to be more mindful of how we use the word love along with the feelings with it and start using it only for the deeper, in-depth reasons it was meant for. Some of us use this same word when we say God is love, but most of the feelings behind this context have been convoluted and confused with lust. Just like being "in love" has been confused with I love the lovemaking you give. Have you noticed that people will say they are "in love" or they love each other but are just dating each other without a true commitment? This is fine if it's a proper courtship, but if it's not, then what is it, really? There is a passage in the Bible that describes the word love in its entirety. When the word love is described in the Bible, it says all the gushy things that make you smile, but it also reads of some things that should make us uncomfortable and honestly look at ourselves.

Like when it says that love isn't self-seeking, when we can be very self-seeking people. Where is the love if we are "in love" but won't commit our lives to this person? Is it because there is something there that is selfishly keeping you, like a condition? When you fell in love, was it just part of the way? Is there another level to fall into? Love is a choice; we choose to love the man or woman we're with. We further solidify that love with the covenant of marriage; getting married is a selfless act. We have to stop using the word love for things that have conditions and no commitment. Here's why. When God says that he loves us, we need to know that the love that God has for us is not like the love from any woman or man. When we dump the word love out to someone, and then we hurt them, and then God's word comes into view, and he says I love you, we miss it. We don't view it the same way it was meant. There can not be I love chocolate, and then I love God in the same breath. This is why healing from the past is so important: so when we feel that true love, we know it's real because we are fully healed and open to receiving it.

The love of God gives peace, as I said before, but it also gives us joy like nothing you could ever find on earth. The love from God keeps us from searching for this lost feeling that we're missing something in life. Have you heard someone ever say there has to be more? Well, there is more, but we'll never find it in the things and people that have conditions for them. Even when someone chooses to love us, it will still come with disappointment, hurt feelings, and sometimes pain. It will never fill us or make us not feel like, at some point, there is something else. That lost feeling is that engagement from God, that connection that we had with him before we were even formed. This is why when you come under the hand of God, you feel peace and joy, and you feel content fully without unsuitable desires. Love is not just love; the love of God is love, and it will conquer all fear, anxiety, loneliness, hurt, pain, mental anguish, loss, and whatever damage has come our way. Whatever void or lack that we feel God will stand in that gap, we just have to open the door and trust in the love and word of the Lord.

We should never miss a chance to be loved, and to be loved eternally for eternity is a grace that withstands all. If God can still love us all like this then he is still on the throne! Hallelujah for that because God lives, and he loves us all.

R. E. P. E. A. T.
resolve. edify. pursue. evolve. amplify. teach.

Chapter 6
God Lives

R. E. P. E. A. T.
resolve. edify. pursue. evolve. amplify. teach.

God Lives
Pursue

There are times when things have come about around me, and I have complained about the devil trying to attack me or stand in the way of my blessing. However, one day, as I was praying, the Lord led me to realize that sometimes we give the enemy too much energy or credit where there shouldn't be. We like to believe God is just love and all the happy things that make us feel good. What we sometimes fail to grasp is that God has dominion over the earth now and forever. Some of the things that we say are the devil is God molding and shaping us with what is needed to succeed or overcome. When I realized this, it made me look at myself. I was able to see things that made me change my speech and thoughts. We give the devil so much credit we sometimes call his name more than we do God. Exhalting his name above the Father as if he has that much control. I hate to say that but examine yourself as well, and you'll see it. God says that he will lift us in due time, but we must be alert of the devil that lurks about, just waiting for an open window or door. So, the only way to cause the destruction that he desires is for us to be open and willing.

R. E. P. E. A. T.
resolve. edify. pursue. evolve. amplify. teach.

God Lives
Pursue

So the next time that you may be going through something, ask yourself after this is done when it's all over, will I be better from it? Will there be a lesson that will evolve you in the end? We have to be careful of where the pressure may be sometimes coming from. God lives, but he allows the devil to dwell in the earth. The devil has no rights to our souls, minds, bodies, or anything unless we open ourselves to him. God was meant to live upon the earth through us, where we have allowed the devil to be. His grace and mercy give us daily life, so let our voices be used by him, and our arms work with his regard. Love someone with his love and grace. Don't allow your body to breed hate and dislike. Don't let your mouth speak obscenities, hurt, or wrong to others. Instead, let God live through you. Let every breath you take be for the one who gives you that breath every day. We should do God this service; he is our father. God wants us to choose him, but with grace and sacrifice, God gives us choice. Imagine lying down asleep in your bed. Imagine all the world doing this. People of all colors, from all backgrounds. When you sleep, your body goes into a comatose state to where you literally are near death.

R. E. P. E. A. T.
resolve. edify. pursue. evolve. amplify. teach.

God Lives
Pursue

Your breathing, but faintly, you could lose oxygen to your brain just like that. Many people die in their sleep just like this; people just go to sleep and never wake up. Are you still imagining the people all around the world? Rich, poor, homeless, kind people, mean people, just people of all races. Asleep. Now imagine that the breath of life comes to each one of them, one by one, to give them the breath of life so that they live another day. Imagine now that same breath being taken away from some of the people you were imagining. Instead of breathing life into them, God takes their breath of life away, and they suffocate and pass away. Gone, just like that.

Even with some of us not choosing God, who has given life and can take it away, every day, we receive the mercy of that breath of life. The only reason we still have life to live is for our creator to be able to help as many as we can along the path of life given, to choose our Father again. God just wants us to live a life of love and submission to him with daily acknowledgment of him, not the devil.

God felt proud that he made such a beautiful earth, and he just wanted to give a piece of his creation to his most incredible creation for the reason of choice, but also to enjoy it, for his children to delight in what he created but not to serve it over him or exalt any other thing or name but his. To not come and indulge in all the things of the earth that would make any father turn his head from us in shame. To be fruitful of all the beauty that was given in the right way that honors such an honorable father. To be proud and joyful looking down on his children with a love that continues to grow with our humble acts of love towards him and each other. When you were little, didn't you want to make your parents proud? To look from the crowd for a smile and see the satisfied smile on their face from all the sacrifice it took to raise you to this moment in your life? How is our heavenly father different? Today! Life was breathed into you because you are able to read this book, right? It is because God lives and is giving us that grace from day to day. What did you do with your breath of life today? How did you live for our father?

How did you allow him to breathe when he allowed you to breathe? Need a change? Do you need to step back and redo some things today? Well, you can't. Time continually moves forward whether you change the digits or not, but going forward, from NOW! We can do better; we can do more. Don't say I'll try from here on; saying you'll try is a cop-out. It suggests that you are limiting the amount of effort that you're going to put toward it. Just do commit because time doesn't wait, and we may not have much time left. Listen, I pray we all have a long life to enjoy the creations of God while on the earth, but it's not promised. So again, I'll try. It is just an excuse, and we will leave it open for us to give partial effort. Do we deserve partial life? Some of us, maybe, lol. I'm just saying, but God gives us full life when he breathes that life into us every day. So, let us give ourselves fully to God and give credit only where it's due. To the living God be all the glory, Amen. God looks upon us daily and gives us all that we need. Don't take my word for it that God lives. Look around you and read the word of God when he says that the birds are not looking for food.

These birds don't have a mind as intricate as ours, but they just know what to do and never worry about their food. Have you ever had a squirrel come up to you asking or looking like they need help? I haven't... Ok. Ok. Seriously, though. God lives in the heavens and throughout the earth because the Spirit of the Lord lives in us. When God created Adam, as I said before, he breathed his soul into him from the heavens, which gave his body life. This is why the answer to whether God lives or not is within us. We carry with us a precious piece, but if we allow the devil to take our soul, then we no longer have that connection.

Are you listening...

R. E. P. E. A. T.
resolve. edify. pursue. evolve. amplify. teach.

God Lives
Pursue

One thing I think we should understand is that the devil speaks too. As long as we're in the world, the devil can speak to anyone open and willing, but not by force. We choose to fuel him by listening; you don't have to be of the world to hear him just fallen or separated from God, even if just for a moment. Yet, God says that his sheep will hear his voice, but we must keep the line of communication open. When someone starts to argue with you, if you don't fuel the fire, how long do you think they'll go on? It's when we fuel that fire by engaging with them or allowing their words to penetrate that we react, and that gives it energy. This is the same for the one who wants to fuel your fire, whether it's harshly or softly. Don't believe that the devil comes only in a rage. The word says that Satan can come to us masquerading as an angel of light, but the key is to be close to God. The closer your relationship with the Father is, the more you'll know who's who. The more peace that you will have that will make the understanding of the words or gestures something that you can see right through.

The critical thing also to differentiate this is knowing who our God is and what he stands for by reading his word. I believe we forget that the devil was close to this whole thing; he was an angel. He knows the Bible just like you may know the Bible. As we've seen throughout history, someone can read the Bible and interpret it in a way that is different from what it means. So sometimes, he can use it to control you, make you believe, or do something completely wrong with the manipulation of the Bible. If I were a scholar and had expert knowledge of something, I could twist it how I wanted to as well; we all could. If you feel like you're hearing from God, ask yourself: does what's being asked or said have anything to do with killing, stealing, or destroying? Does it have anything to do with hate? These terms are universally vast, so just think of those when trying to see if this is God. The devil, even with the knowledge, has only so much room, so if you look at the broader picture, he does the same things. We've heard that history repeats itself well, and so does he. We all do what works, right? Well, this has been true for him since the start of Eve.

See, God is love in the literal sense of the word. Love has a deepness that goes a long way into its meaning. Ironically, hate works the same way. It can run very deep and even be persuasive. You need to take a moment and look up the definition of love and hate. Then, come back to read and understand more of what I'm trying to convey. God is love in every sense of the word. The devil is hate in the literal sense of the word as well; it works the same way, just with opposite desires. So if you feel as if you're hearing from God, and it has anything to do with love, it is a means to prosper you and give you a future. That's God all day, love! Run with that as far as you can! Lol. If you hear your "spirit" or " subconscious" tell you something, and it's the opposite of love. Run and pray, darling. That's the trick of the devil! You have to have a close relationship to truly hear God's voice. Be friends with him! Let God fill you up with his love and grace! Work with him every day! Talk to him about the small stuff. You'll be more willing with the big stuff. The more you lean and ask or speak to God. The more love you'll have. God lives! He can hear your prayers, your cries, your anxiousness.

The more love you have inside, the more beautiful you'll become in all ways of beauty. You'll have so much that you will want to give just as much. You'll have so much to give because God will make sure you have what you need to do what you need as long as it's for his house and not to make things that are already horrible worse. Like it's been said, for me and my house, listen! I remember reading one day in school about how essential oxygen is and how much we need it. How nothing harmful can live in an oxygenated environment. Well, get yourself oxygenated. We need that! Let God breathe into you. We need that to just be right, to just be in a better alignment. What's that song? How can I breathe with no air? Well, you can't. Instead, we should be singing that other song Breathe into me, oh Lord, because he lives!

R. E. P. E. A. T.

resolve. edify. pursue. evolve. amplify. teach.

Chapter 7
Guard Your Sense

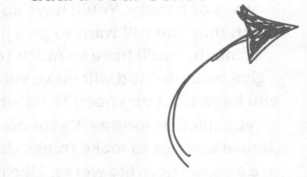

Have you ever watched the Television with the sound off? You should try it. The sound makes all the difference. There are people in places at companies who spend so much time coming up with ways to tantalizingly lure you into things that click on your brain that indulge or intrigue you to want. Don't forget that we have five senses. God says to be careful of what you allow your ears to hear and your eyes to see. God knows how important your sensors are and how powerfully they can affect you, stir you, or move you. Why don't we know? The people who use them against us indeed do. We are always guarding things that are important to us, like our children and our essential material possessions. We protect these things sometimes with our lives. Why won't we do the same for the one thing we have control over, our minds, the birthright to choose our ability to think or to decide? There are constant reminders that remind us of things in our lives that are of importance, like trial and error, obstacles, and death. We go through things so that we can constantly be reminded, humbled, and centered as much as we have to distract us from life itself.

R. E. P. E. A. T.
resolve. edify. pursue. evolve. amplify. teach.

Things like these bring us to a somewhat humility to be grounded in what's important in life. Why wait? Why only have that reality when things get tough? How do you deal? How do you stay centered? By consistently being prepared. Mind, body, and Spirit. Just like you save for a rainy day, you have to do the same for the importance of the only life you receive. Pray all day, every day. Nothing big, not hours of prayer, just a conversation with God throughout the day like we do with ourselves. I know you do it we all do. Arm yourself like you arm your house with guns and alarms. It's vital for you. Why not live this only life that you receive in peace and physical harmony? God says to seek him, and he will give us perfect peace. Peace that surpasses all understanding. That's great! Sign me up! We all say, man, if I could go back in time and do this or do that. Listen, if something is broken, fix it! If you're building a house and you have to take everything down and rebuild from the beginning because you missed an important step, then rebuild! If you don't fix it, everything will fall over anyway. So, of course, you'd rebuild; you'd start over. Do it! Do it! Why not? Rebuild.

Now that you know more about what to do, it shouldn't take you long to get back to the spot you need to be. Restart, reset, reevaluate, rebuild! Bigger and better! You'd do it for any materialistic thing you have. Now, I'm telling you to do it for something far more significant that's way more valuable than you can put a price on, yourself; Do it. Do it for you and your eternal life. Why not? You're worth it! Please believe that. Sit in silence sometimes. Just look and listen in mute at the world around you. Meditate on the importance of it all, in silence in the shower or something like that. I get out most thoughts and ideas to God in this time. Go to the beach. That's another one of my favorite spots. I believe God speaks through water, but that's just me. I go where I can hear my Spirit and hash things out with God and myself to get resolutions. Without this resolve, there's no evolving, and we resort to these other things that we believe give us insight.

Life is an embrace, an embrace of faith. Whether we know it or not, we practice it every day. Faith is just having complete trust and belief in something.

When our brains tell our bodies to walk, speak, cry, yell, or whatever, we have complete trust and complete faith that our bodies will be able to do just that. This is why when I hear people saying that they don't trust or have faith, I say yes, we all have faith. We embrace faith all the time and don't give it a second thought. Some people look at getting older like it's the plague! Why don't we embrace it? It's a tremendous accomplishment to have made it so far. You've survived. You've lived through some things, you have a story to tell, and you were saved for a reason. Otherwise, so many people wouldn't have had that same fate. Why'd you make it?

Embrace that wisdom, that grace upon your life. Listen, I understand that some things are hard for our physical minds just to embrace and be ok with. If you lose someone that you were close to, it's going to be challenging to embrace. Eventually, we come to terms with these things through time, but it can still be difficult. I'm merely speaking about the embrace of daily things that we can not control and having the embrace of faith so we do not have to worry about them. Worrying changes nothing. All things that we can not control stay the same, even in our times of worry. So what's the point? This total trust that we have on a daily needs to be the same faith that we give God. If we make it to tomorrow, where will our faith lie?

Chapter 8
Out Our Mouths, The Heart Speaks

We don't talk enough. On some of the
days when I was writing this book, I had to
be up early, like 6:15 type early, or stay up
till then, lol. I'm not a late sleeper, but
this was early for me. So I would stay up
late and then have to write in the wee am
hours when the house was still. I would be
complain type tired if you know you
know. But when you have something that
you're being led to do, you need to do it!
Don't get me wrong, you have to be sure
that your Spirit is right, but you'll know if
it's God. We must do things in the order of
God, but God can use anyone willing. So if
you know God, I mean have a relationship
with him, and you have the wisdom and
knowledge to help the youth, your co-
worker, a woman, a man, or a stranger.
Tell it! Teach! We don't talk enough for
the right reasons. You know, tell the truth
and shame the devil! When we have open
dialogue, it's like confessional, helping us
to bring air and light to the truth so that
we may be healed or protected from it.
So, tell it even if it hurts them or you.
Lack of communication has never helped
us. Never. The little family secrets that
never get told but are just buried. Stop it,
tell it, heal from it, and move forward.

R. E. P. E. A. T.
resolve. edify. pursue. evolve. amplify. teach.

Out Our Mouths, The Heart
Speaks
Evolve

Some of us will argue with our spouse or anyone that we care for to the death. Yet, when it comes to verbal expression or enlightening someone, we all fall short. Too afraid or too embarrassed or feel like it's a waste of time. We need to stop it! Do it even if you think it's a waste of time. God won't move you to speak to someone if he feels like it's a waste of time. Even if you feel like it's not getting through or helping, something is, there's resignation somewhere; I know because I've been on both sides of it. I'm not taking credit for anything that God has led me to do. It's all by his grace, and we need to do things by his grace even if we don't get immediate recognition. We just need to be obedient; otherwise, we're missing the point anyway. Sometimes, it's just about being obedient to what God is telling us to do. God is just periodically checking our hearts, making sure we stay on track and if we will listen to see what we can be trusted with. So when that time comes, he knows he can count on us. Whoever is a parent should be able to relate. Tell it! Teach! We don't speak enough.

R. E. P. E. A. T.
resolve. edify. pursue. evolve. amplify. teach.

Out Our Mouths, The Heart Speaks
Evolve

For the ones who have children, big or small, or you're looking to have them in the future, practice this! God loves the innocent child! LOVES! If we have been blessed with a child and didn't do right with that gift, we will have to answer to God for this. So, no matter how trivial the conversation is to us, we need to take time to listen to our children because the wisdom we have may help them. Our children may come to us and say one thing, but then, because we have wisdom, we recognize something in what they've said that needs more attention. God plays no games with the innocent child. Our children are a reflection of us. The nerve they may hit is a mirrored reflection!

They are also one of the biggest blessings that God gives to us so that we can develop things such as patience and being slow to anger. These things help us and make us better in life, but other things keep us from having a better life. We need to know both sides to be better individually for the example being seen. The four things God told me that keep us from so much in life are unforgiveness, pride, fear, and patience. Now I know what some of you are thinking; I could add so much more to that list. But it's like the definition that God gives of love. Those four words go so much deeper on another level than we ever have thought of. Go and take a moment to look up the definition of each one...

Do you see how many avenues they can go? When you read each word, it can take you to so many places in your life. We must not let unforgiveness, pride, fear, or lack of patience keep us from having much-needed conversations. Create opportunities to talk with our Father, spouse, children, family, or just people who need an ear or heart for wisdom. Do it with no conditions or intentions but with just love in your heart. We must speak to be heard.

Chapter 9
Hop-To-It! 🎵🎵

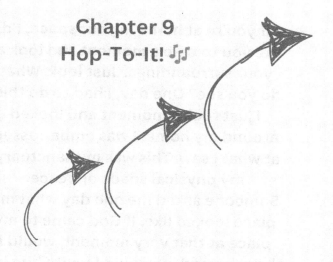

R. E. P. E. A. T.
resolve. edify. pursue. evolve. amplify. teach.

Hop-To-It♪♪
Amplify

If you're at home in your space, I'd like you to take a moment and look at your surroundings. Just look. What do you see? One day, I had to do this; I just took a moment and looked around my home. I was embarrassed at what I saw. This was my sanctuary, my physical space of peace. Someone asked me one day what my place looked like. If God came to my place at that very moment, would I be ashamed, or would I invite him in with open arms? I looked at them; I had to think about that. The answer at that time was no, but I don't remember what I said. I probably lied and said yes, my house is always tidy. It wasn't; I allowed what I felt internally to translate into my physical space. I asked God what I could do. I was so overwhelmed just trying to work and keep it all together on my own. I was just going one day at a time at this point, sometimes moment to moment.

R. E. P. E. A. T.
resolve. edify. pursue. evolve. amplify. teach.

Hop-To-It♪♫
Amplify

So, I had a conversation with God before I got into the shower on a Tuesday. For whatever reason, I can always hear my Spirit very clearly in the shower. My Spirit said to take it one day at a time; it is just that simple. There's something to do each day always to make your space look its best. I looked around and knew that it would take some time to get things at their best, but I was determined to have that place where I could feel relaxed and comfortable and where I could have anyone over without shame, including God. So here's the list that was created for my household that helped me to keep things tidy all week. I'm sharing it with you in hopes that you can make your physical space better as well. I'm going to explain each day. This came straight from my Holy Spirit. My prayer is that it possibly helps give you a start in a more balanced direction than before.
Feel free to read these and do them one day at a time if you'd like.

R. E. P. E. A. T.
resolve. edify. pursue. evolve. amplify. teach.

Me Monday: it's important to spend time with yourself. Your surroundings looking their best is important, yet so are you. No matter what your body or how your face looks to some people, we are all perfectly made. Taking care of whatever God gave you is essential to a healthy life and feeling great in addition. It was once said to me that your outer appearance reflects how you feel about yourself on the inside. I understand that some people don't like the way they look but it's time out for that! Embrace what God gave you and make the most of life with joy in your heart! I'm that person who can always tell if someone has altered themselves with surgery, cut, snipped, or plumped up something. These aren't needed; we are ALL beautifully made. The devil may have convinced you otherwise every time you look into the mirror, but there's manipulation involved. The devil has us thinking there's perfection on this earth. God says there is no perfect person, and he means that. God made you perfectly in his image, so altering yourself only sometimes changes your mind for the better or the worse.

R. E. P. E. A. T.
resolve. edify. pursue. evolve. amplify. teach.

Hop-To-It♫
Amplify

God doesn't make mistakes. The so-called mistakes that you feel you have wouldn't be a factor if something or someone in this world didn't tell you what beauty is. Beauty is in the eye of who truly sees you, and the only vision that counts is God's and the spouse he has for you. If God is for you and the way he made you, whoever can be against that shouldn't get your energy to care anyway. These types of people are some of the ugliest people if you could see them beyond their physical bodies. No one is physically perfect. We all have flaws, 2 or 3 or more. So what? We are proportionate in the exact way in the same form that we were meant for. We all have one arm or leg longer, an eye or ear higher, but I bet we have perfect balance.

R. E. P. E. A. T.
resolve. edify. pursue. evolve. amplify. teach.

Even if we don't have more than most, it doesn't mean we are less worthy of a me day. So this day is dedicated to whatever that means for you. If it's doing your hair, this day, make it your hair day, your nails, your feet, or a day of reflection. Male or female, do it for you; this is your day. On me Monday, my first day, I just spent time with myself. I didn't have a lot of money, so I just went for a walk around my neighborhood and looked around. I washed my hair, took care of my nails, and watched a film by myself. I spent some time with my family. That's what was important for me. Whatever makes you feel great, elevates you, and doesn't harm you, do it. Focus on you. Me Monday.

**The next day
Tuesday is,**
Toilet Tuesday: I know this is everyone's least favorite job to do. On our first toilet Tuesday, I was so overwhelmed. It was so much to do after slacking on it for some time. No, it wasn't this wretched mess, but it wasn't company-ready either. The first week is usually the hardest until you get into a routine. Even though it's not the most fun, it's just as important as taking care of your person. Remember, this is where you go to get cleaned up and look fresh. You're discarding all your dirt, brushing your teeth, and doing your hair. By the grace of God, this is where you start your day. So you shouldn't feel clean unless you're cleaning yourself in a clean environment. So, on this day, I went to that famous store where things only used to cost a dollar, and I got all of what I needed to make my bathroom look nice and tidy. There can be so much that we neglect in our bathrooms that we should continue to address to keep down germs. For example, why are the corners on the floor where the shower and the floor meet so dirty with lent hair and dirt? I took some old shirts that I wasn't going to wear, and I poured bleach on them in my bath.

Then I let them sit on those corners while I worked on the mirror, bath, toilet, countertop, sinks, and floor. After I was done, I went back, took a wet cloth, and wiped it. I got those easers for the wall, and I cleaned that, too. (You can also use an old shirt or towel with soap and water) It took me nearly 2 hours to get things clean, but I turned on some hop-to-it music and had some fun dancing around while I cleaned. So turn on something and get to work! The next day, when I went into my bathroom, I felt better about getting up in the morning. Having a cleaned bathroom like that just made my day start right. It was like being at a new place with a new place smell, lol. I can't explain it better. You'll have to see for yourself after you do your bathroom on toilet Tuesday. You'll know just what I mean.

R. E. P. E. A. T.
resolve. edify. pursue. evolve. amplify. teach.

Hop-To-It♫
Amplify

**The next day
Wednesday is,
Wipe out Wednesday: All day long, we're collecting germs because we live on a decaying earth, and there is so much dust. My first day doing this took me a minute! (Not literally) There is always dust and germs lingering, just waiting for us to get sick. The last place that we should get sick is our home. With company over and children in and out of the house, this is a must. Someone had food on their hands, then touched a knob or a light switch, and now they have food on them. Someone sneezed and now transferred those germs to whatever they sneezed on. If you have children, you know exactly what I mean. Having a dust-free environment will help your health to breathe better with ease, and keeping your environment mostly germ-free will keep sickness down. The health of your environment where you live is important for your body and mind. So, on this day, we wiped out everything: germs, clutter, and anything else that needed wiping out. We wiped walls, knobs on all doors, windowpanes, blinds, ceiling fans, and whatever was needed in the structure of our layout.**

We even wiped some of the bottles, like the mustard and ketchup, that had whatever was dripping from the top. Just take off that topper and rinse it under the water. Get that dried-up stuff off that top, at least for your first wipeout Wednesday. The next time you use it, you'll love the way it makes you feel. Sometimes it's the small things. Getting something from a clean item makes a difference. My family and I wiped everywhere that we thought that dust germs and dirt were. It's also a great way to spend family time. If you have kids, you can get them involved, no matter their age. Just notice I said kids, not babies. If they can walk, my Nana says they can help; not much help, though, lol. Washing clothes on this day of the week was also eased into this day when things became easier to finish. This took us a while the first time, but we turned on that hop-to-it music, and we had fun. When Wipe Out Wednesday was over, I felt like I could go anywhere in the house, nearly germ and dirt-free. If you have the money, also look up some plants that complement your environment and are great for giving you more oxygen to wipe out things in the air. Wipe out Wednesday.

R. E. P. E. A. T.
resolve. edify. pursue. evolve. amplify. teach.

Hop-To-It♪♫
Amplify

Next day
Thursday is,
T. A. Z. Thursday: With the rest of the house being Nice and clean and almost germ-free, I was ready for the next thing to get organized. I went back to that store that I like where everything used to be a dollar, and I got little bins and things that could help me organize and find things more easily. It's something about being able just to get what you need when you need it. Everything has its place. When you go into someone's house or see someone's vehicle, if they have just stuff everywhere, it can sometimes put you in a funk, so imagine what it does if you're around it every day. Our mind tends to be what we see daily, so if it's cluttered, then so is our mind. Just cluttered and all over the place, not able to concentrate. This clutter does no good for our minds or Spirits. In some cases, it can cause depression. If you've ever looked at someone's home and were bragging about how nice and organized it was, there are some things I'm sure they did to get there. The only difference between you and them is that they made it up in their mind to get things in order and followed through.

So this is something that you can do. When everything is in its place, you can think more clearly and not be so turned around. This is the time when you have to be honest with yourself and just let things go. We all have things just lying about, like old papers and clothes, that we'll never give away or wear. These are things that we keep thinking about if we ever need it later, we'll have it, and years later, we still have it but don't need it. Things that when you find, you're like, I didn't know I had this! When did I buy that? So, I think it's safe to say, um, you don't need that. Sell it or give it away to someone in need. You didn't even know it was there. You haven't needed it thus far, so I'm sure you'll be ok if you let it go. Let me get a little deep for a moment. Sometimes, things that we hold on to may have sentimental value. What value is more precious than the memory you have? (not to be insensitive at all) God doesn't want us to be so caught up in these material things that we have in our possession that they become of more value than things that do. The things of this earth that are material in actuality have no real value. They can decay, burn, and wither away, including our bodies.

R. E. P. E. A. T.

But that's for another chapter. So when it comes to things that we're holding on to, whether it's something dear and sentimental or something that's just "life" for you, things of this world on this earth that can tarnish and wither away weren't meant for you to idolize. By no means am I saying every little thing needs to go; some things may keep you in good Spirit just to look at them, but for the ones that can be let go of, let it go. If you think about it, why does God give us a memory? Not just for the day-to-day tasks but think about how far our memories can go. As far back as you being a child and in some cases further than that. God knew we would need the ability to hold certain moments close with the understanding that things tarnish, break, and fade away. Think about all the minor incidents and exciting times or even some of the emotional times that you can think of throughout your life so far. You should be amazed. So, turn on that hop-to-it music that gets you going, love, and have that declutter organize my life in mind.

Now, in full transparency, the first time we did this, it took me all of Thursday and some of Friday morning. For some people, it could take a couple of Thursdays or even more. Don't worry about how long it will take. Just do it! Your life will be better for it! On Thursday, we went through every room and cleaned and organized it. Vacuumed, mopped, threw away unnecessary things (wink), took bins that we had gotten to store things, and organized for the season. We took the other stuff we bought to organize and gave everything a home. Seriously, when I first did this, I was overwhelmed by the disorganized spot that we'd created. I didn't know where to start, so I just took everything down and out and then put it all back together with organization. One room at a time, whatever was needed, we tidied all areas of our home. T. A. Z. Thursday.

R. E. P. E. A. T.
resolve. edify. pursue. evolve. amplify. teach.

Hop-To-It♫
Amplify

Next Day
Friday is,
Fridge Friday: At my house, the weekend is when I cook. I'll cook during the week as well, but not five or 6-course meals. This is also the time when things need to be replenished and when we have to reload and clean our refrigerator. One of the most embarrassing things is to have old food in your refrigerator, but it's even worse when there's a smell attached to it. You shouldn't have to stress at the last minute to cram a week's worth of cleaning into an hour or two. You should be ready to have over family and friends and be able to say there are some beverages in the refrigerator to help yourself without later thinking about what they felt about your dirty fridge. You want people to come by and really like your place; you want people to see God first in all that you do and you. This is also the day we go to the market. So on this day, Fridge Friday, it's out with the old and in with the new. We make sure things are not expired; this is also the time to tidy up those bottles that have spilled over for the first time or again. With everyone pitching in, we would have this done in about 20 minutes; then, we'll be off to the market.

We go to the market and get what we need to replenish the refrigerator for the week. I've learned not to over-buy so that we don't waste or overeat, so having a plan only for the week is always good. When it's there, sometimes we eat just cause. Instead, I think it's better to do other things with idle time. We get our favorite fruit, veggies for salad, dinner items, breakfast items, and snack stuff for the week. I invested in some storage containers so that when we get home from the market, I can wash or chop the fruit and vegetables to store them away. Having easy access helps keep it fresh till the end of the week as well. I also do this with sliced meat to allow my family easy access to make sandwiches. So now we're set for the weekend and the next coming week. Having the things to help replenish your body gives you the balance needed for other areas to function well in your life. However, you can make this happen by buying or being blessed with it, do it. Food is a needed source of life; if done to nourish and replenish our bodies, it will serve its purpose. So, take pride in doing so. This is the blessing that I pray over the food that I'm blessed to receive, and also a prayer for those who have not. Fridge Friday

**Next day
Saturday is,
Slack Saturday: After all that
work during the week. You
deserve a day to rest. I'm not
sure why Saturday comes as a
day of rest in my Spirit, but it
does. We do not all have no work
on this day, but rest where you
can if you do. Take time off your
phone and devices, and when
you get home, rest. Now that all
the other days are done, you
have a clean house to do it in. Or,
if all is well at home, you can go
out and enjoy the weather, spend
time with your family or friends,
etc. When you come back home,
it'll feel great to relax in a clean
environment. It's a day just to
relax and catch up. When you
work so hard through the week,
you should allow yourself some
rest time.**

R. E. P. E. A. T.
resolve. edify. pursue. evolve. amplify. teach.

You can sleep in if you can, or just put your feet up. Rest is a great way to rejuvenate the body. We heal when we sleep, and this is why my family takes vitamins at night when they can be beneficial. Rest keeps a balance; not too much, but just enough. So, on this day, Slack Saturday. Don't be afraid to lose yourself in rest and relaxation. It doesn't have to be sleep; some people feel rested when they're reading a book or doing a puzzle. Wear comfortable clothes and do that thing that brings you great love, relaxation, and rest. For my family, we generally just hang out as a family on this day around the house or wherever. We'll watch a film and talk about it, play a game together, or we all do our own thing. Slack means slack, so this is the day to enjoy whatever gives you that. So slack Saturday.

Next day
Sunday is,
Serve Sunday: After a day of rest, time to yourself, shopping, and cleaning, it's time to give back. On this day, we think of community. There are people out there who need that community. We all do. Think about how blessed you've been all week in being able to do whatever you've done. Think about the people who couldn't. There are people right now in your very community who are going through things. That may need our help. So, this is the day that you serve someone else. Look around you. There is someone in need. You don't have to always go to your city to feed the homeless, even though that's also a great idea. People around you may have been recently ill, got injured, and can't cut their grass, or several things. There are people in your community who may have just lost someone and need someone just to say God loves you to light that fire back in them. Go pray with them. They may be a single mother and need a man to come by and play with their son (with Godly intentions). If you're a single man as well, who knows where God can lead that! JS. Lol

R. E. P. E. A. T.

resolve. edify. pursue. evolve. amplify. teach.

If you are a teacher on this day for just an hour or two, find someone in your community to Tudor to help them learn in a better way. You could set up a game with the local kids who don't have their parents there on the weekend because they work or they're missing a parent. All you need is a ball and some grass. Adults or teens, give your wisdom to a kid trying to figure it out. I'm just throwing ideas because I know how easy it is to excuse yourself from the equation of being able to serve. We all have something to give that can be used to serve others. If your gift is financial, then financially bless someone in need. We have talents that God has gifted us to give to someone else. These things can be ongoing. People should know they can come to you for help if need be. Kids should be able to go to you for advice when there's nowhere else they can turn. Whatever your talent, whatever your wisdom, give it. Pray first for discernment of who, where, and when because God will not lead us astray. It only takes your time; who knows whose life you can change or help. You could keep a lost child from committing suicide.

R. E. P. E. A. T.
resolve. edify. pursue. evolve. amplify. teach.

Hop-To-It♫
Amplify

You can't tell what people are going through from the outside. You have to go deeper than the surface. Yet once you break that barrier by just giving your time, knowledge, or skills, you'll be surprised at what people open up about when they feel your genuine intentions. Start in your community and get other adults or teenagers involved. The elders are meant to lead the children. Only do things that you are comfortable with; like I said, always pray first and be led by the Holy Spirit. God is aware that times are different, but the grace and mercy upon his child haven't changed. Go in the name of God and know that you are protected. You can start small; I recommend it. Some people don't want to talk to others because they may be shy about rejection. You can't live or love like this, not as a child of God. We must be doers of the word and not just listeners. As long as you are living and have breath in your body, you must do something more than just for yourself and your family. Sometimes when you're helping someone else you can also wind up helping yourself.

R. E. P. E. A. T.
resolve. edify. pursue. evolve. amplify. teach.

This is a win-win; as much as you give, you will receive because God will replenish what you need. Great things come back around like a boomerang. On this day, Serve Sunday, we give to whoever will receive. If we see someone in need, we help in the best way we can. God says not to boast, so I won't get into all that my family and I will do and have done. Just think about serving on this day; take time to serve God on this day by praying and spending time with him doing his will. Be sure to do this; it's a necessity for your balance. Serve Sunday is my most fulfilling day. ...and R. E. P. E. A. T.

Chapter 10
The Important Trio

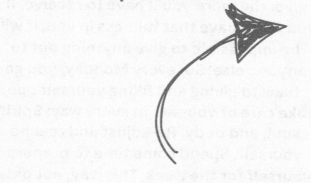

After you have given, you must now be replenished, so that's why we will come back to me Monday. The more that you give, the more you'll have to receive. If you don't have that fullness in you, it will be impossible to give anything out to anyone else. So, every Monday, you go back to giving and filling yourself up. Take care of yourself in every way: Spirit, soul, and body. Re-adjust and realine yourself. Spend some time to prepare yourself for the week. This way, not only will your soul and heart be replenished to give love, but you'll also take care of your body so that you will have the energy to endure physically. Do you see how that works together? It was something that was given to me by the Holy Spirit that helped me when I needed it most, and I'm blessed to share it with you. I know that this will help and allow you to get things in order, give you balance, and align you in the way that you should be. Some of us are out of alignment and just need to be re-adjusted; some of us are body first, soul next, and Spirit last. Being out of alignment steers you off course and keeps you going the wrong way; you're just all over the place like a car that's out of alignment.

When you have that balance, you can take your hands off the wheel, and it will stay on track. Who wouldn't want to have that balance? Ask yourself, do you have that now, or do you feel a bit off balance? Feel like you are all over the place? Feel like you keep going left when you should be going right? So let's fix that, love! How long have you tried it the wrong way or been out of alignment? Has your way worked? My way never did. So, I had to ask myself these questions one day and then humble myself enough to be honest with my answers. When I did this, I was able to ask for help. Since I had no one who could physically be there to help me, I called on the one person with whom I knew I always felt peace with. Who I felt always listened, who gave me sound advice, and who made that empty feeling I felt always go away. Some of you may have guessed it. Some of you may have not, but it was God. I know it sounds cliche, yet it's not; it's just the truth. I wish I could say that it was my mother, siblings, children, my hubby, or my best friend, but it wasn't.

R. E. P. E. A. T.
resolve. edify. pursue. evolve. amplify. teach.

There's a reason why God says that people will hurt you or disappoint you, so don't put your trust in man. It's true. Not men, as in that man who hurt you, but he never deserved your love in the first place; God means mankind, so that's anyone. I'm not saying you shouldn't trust; I'm just saying that you can't put your full trust in mankind. People have their things going on most of the time internally, so when it comes to something that we want them just to know or for which we set high expectations, we can count on them disappointing us and hurting us in some way. It's just how human we are. If we are honest with ourselves, we're one of these same people. When I went to God, I genuinely went to him as if I were speaking to a dear friend or a close relative. Just openly and honestly seeking help. Trying to understand and navigate life. I was so lost and messed up, and I needed guidance; I just felt out of alignment. So, I just asked why I was so lost; I felt like Dorothy. Seriously! I just asked that simple question in that way. Then I remembered someone telling me one day to be slow to anger, slow to speak, and quick to listen.

So, after I asked God this simple question. I shut up and sat there in silence, waiting to hear back from him. I repeated in my head some scriptures that I had heard over the years to keep my mind on him while I waited for an answer. I sat there for a good minute, but I was so frustrated that I had it made up in my mind that I was going to sit there until I got through because I needed my question answered. The moment I was going to ask God again, I began to hear his voice. I don't know about you, but my mind sometimes works so complicated that when God speaks to me, he'll also bring things back to my memory to give me mental imagery of exactly what he means, almost like a play with words like a narrator. So, he began to do this as I listened. There is no short version to explain this fully, so hopefully, you are patiently reading this. What God shared with me on this day. It will always stay with me and made so much sense. As complicated as we think God may be in a lot of ways, we complicate God too much, but. God said this. With imagery, maybe because I'm a visual person, picture this with me.

When we were first conceived in our mother's womb. We grow in a way that we depend on her, but we also have blind faith in innocence and expectancy. Like how we look at animals. They don't have the brilliant, complex minds that we have, yet they know exactly what to do. They do exactly what they were brought here to do, and they all have a purpose, whether small or big, to help life keep a balance of things. When you think about it. We all came from being in the womb, relying on the mother to give us what we need and the body automatically knowing exactly what to do to grow. The only difference is that we don't stay in this state. When we're in the womb, we're vulnerable to anything. Our noses are plugged, and we're surrounded by our mother's blood and water. Yet, we don't panic, and we don't drown ourselves like we would if we were going through this at this very moment. We trusted blindly, and we expected with full expectation, expected protection, and we were protected. This is where we had our most comfort on this earth with no care of the world.

R. E. P. E. A. T.
resolve. edify. pursue. evolve. amplify. teach.

The Important Trio
Teach

The moment we're born and take our first breath, as close as we were to being so expecting without doubt and trusting blindly, we start to journey away from that. Have you seen a baby when they are first born? How is it that we know how to cry and communicate without being taught? It's just like animals. They may not have a soul, yet there is something that guides them into doing exactly as they should. When we are in the womb, we are so close to God. We have that comfort, that automatic knowing, that blind trust, that full expectancy for life as we know it to be at that time. So we do and act without a care because we have that perfect peace. We come on a clean slate. Once a baby is born, you can still see in some ways how we're still linked to God by looking at how similarly they all act. I know we usually think our baby is somehow different from what they do. We brag about it and get so amazed by it. When someone says oh, my baby does that, we look like, not like, my baby. Like how they smile in their sleep. People have said that they're playing with the angels.

This may be true. Or they're remembering their life with God and remembering how great God is. They all do this. You don't have to teach them to be happy or to have joy. Yet, God is all about love to prosper you and not harm or hurt you. Go figure, right? How many times have we said or heard I wish they could stay this innocent? You know what that says? We know that this world will soon turn them into something else. After God showed me this, he showed me how we choose to stray away. God showed me first how delicately innocent we are and how we don't need to be shown how to trust with expectancy. How much happiness can we have without anyone having to make us laugh or give us a bunch of material things? The love that was given from the start shows on the outside because we were filled on the inside. Parents, this is why it is so important to get it right! That's why children are a gift: being a parent comes with so much power and should be taken seriously. If you've been able to raise kids like I have been fortunate to do, then you have witnessed the power of choice on another level.

Even if you haven't, you can go back to when you were a child or teen and remember. When our babies start to see things around them, the people around them, and the objects around them as they are meant to learn from, sometimes they learn the wrong things. They are doing what they are meant to do and using the brain that God has given to them, but under the influence of the environment. Then, after becoming a toddler and learning the word no, they realize they have a choice. If you've noticed, the moment they become independent by crawling or walking, they slowly stop with that innocent smile in their sleep. The smile is different now. This smile that they may have now is a happy smile rather than a joyful, not a care-in-the-world type of smile. As your relationship changes with them, so does the closeness that we've all, at some point, shared with God. They become so consumed with life and the offerings of the world they see that they start to slowly forget where they came from. When I look at my now 2-year-old, who is so intrigued by everything, I see it, and rightfully so because she's experiencing all this for the first time.

R. E. P. E. A. T.

resolve. edify. pursue. evolve. amplify. teach.

Yet, she's also realizing that she has a choice, so because she's having so much fun learning with the things around her, she forgets to go toilet or fights her sleep so she doesn't miss a thing. My child mimics me; the way that I speak and my mannerisms, just like in the womb, they learn from what we feed them. Once they get older and gain more independence and a mind of their own, they start to stray from you and your teachings. If you've noticed, the more independent you become as an individual, or the more your child becomes independent, the bigger the separation. If you truly think about it, just as we have, they stray from God first. The one from whom we were created. So we shouldn't feel so bad that they also stray from us. If you truly think about it even further than that. Once they stray so far in life, you think they'll never return, yet they always do. Why is that? Depending on your life experience or how old you are, so have we. They always come back. Even if they come back after you've gone, they come back. Something always draws them back from where they came to the source of their beginning.

R. E. P. E. A. T.

resolve. edify. pursue. evolve. amplify. teach.

How many of you have done this or had a son or daughter come back to you and seek your help and guidance or say you were right? How many times have they done this just to go back into the wrong thing eventually? Let me help you understand as I'm sitting in my closet. God revealed so much to me in just a couple of minutes. Then, as I sat there to comprehend all of what was given to me. I asked for understanding. So, my Holy Spirit then came to me to help me understand it all. Where we fall short is that we miss opportunities. As I've said before, there are four things that keep you from so much in life: unforgiveness, patience, fear, and pride. These things come into play at different times for different reasons. Because we consume and hold on to these things so strongly, we forget about the one thing that has given us perfect peace from the start. We allow these things to overlap into a ball of junk that stands in the way of the most intimate thing that we all once shared. Love. This beautiful word comes from God. I can't even begin to tell you how deep the meaning is.

Instead, I'll give you a bit of work to do on your Me Monday. Pick up the Bible, read 1 Corinthians 13 about love, and don't just read it. Dissect it, go through each word that defines the word love, and look at the definitions for them. This all comes back to God! So when your child comes back to you for guidance, it's because they have searched the world and feel like they are missing something. Feeling lost and trying to find what's missing, indulging in drugs, sex, self-harm, or all types of religion because maybe God is not real and they've been lied to. They've been in love, idolized themselves or someone else, and listened to the wrong type of music. Trying out things that they may have never done, just out there in the world, seeking something, anything to fill the missing void. Maybe this child is you, not knowing that it's you because of what you have or how old you are, that you've been stuck in this section of life with immature love. Now, going back to what God was showing me before about how we are when we are in the womb, how content we are, and how we stray so far from it.

How we no longer lean on the comfort of not-a-care in the world with expectancy to be loved, fed, and protected. Then go back to where you or a loved one is right now. Have you been feeling empty, unloved, unprotected? Have you been feeling like a piece is missing from life and have been on the hunt for it? If you don't know what that piece is by now, let me tell you. We've gone high, low, forward, backward, and from side to side just to come back to where we started. Whichever side you're on, whether the parent or the child, where we miss it is that we didn't go back far enough. The piece that you're missing is further than your family or your mother. That perfect peace that you've been going through everything to find that brought you right back to the start is what you're missing. It's something that you'll never be able to find in mankind or any temporary object that can decay or tarnish. You'll only be in the womb with perfect peace like you were before by regaining that blind trust and expectation in life. Only with going back just a bit further and coming back into that love that you first had with God.

That comfort that you felt from the start. The humility to completely be dependent on everything you need to survive this life. The trust that you wouldn't drown in your surroundings or panic from the darkness. The belief of just believing with all you had that things were going to be ok. The loving natural innocence of love and forgiveness we shared when you were a baby. The smile in your sleep, the joy on your face, and just thinking of how great God is. That love that surpassed your surroundings and all understanding of anything that you could have been in danger of or that could have been done to you. That love you had that sadly left when someone who was sick with the devil came to hurt and rob you of or destroy your innocence; innocence where you loved without judgment. We can learn so much from our children or from when we were children. This is what we have all missed. This piece gives us peace; it's God, the Holy name of Yahuah! Only when we come back to this peace will we truly find what we've always needed and longed for on a daily. We shouldn't have to wait.

When people say rest in peace, we should rest in God, who will give us perfect peace right now before our time is cut short. When you figure it out, and you have this better understanding. You do what? R. E. P. E. A. T! Lol. As much as needed. When you're blessed with the opportunity of your child coming back to you, mend your relationship. Let's be the child coming back to our father to mend our relationship that got lost in translation from life. We all have this lack in our lives, and it's time to fill it. Here is your needed Trio...

There are things that God put into place to help us, like angels and the Holy Spirit. Remember when you were reading about alignment and balance? Well, here's the order again: Spirit, Soul, and Body. Your Spirit, your Holy Spirit, should be above all things except your peace (God). This keeps us grounded and looking at things with different eyes. Our Holy Spirit has lived in us since the time God formed us in the womb. Your Holy Spirit is there to be your guide, your voice sometimes, and your spiritual strength.

R. E. P. E. A. T.

We need this strength more than our physical body strength. It is important. It taps into that language and that commutation with God that we can't reach sometimes with our mouths. It gives us discernment on things that we may not be able to see. It's our Spiritual strength. The closest thing that we have to God without actually being in heaven. It's the purest part of this trilogy that we possess to gain a deeper understanding of our reality. You'll have to be open to it; you'll have to let go of yourself fully, like diving into a pool or on a bed. Just let go and allow your guide to lead you. It's in the middle of our soul, the pit of our emotions. It's like a filtration system, filtering out where things need to go and keeping that balance between the two. It's needed to help you decipher what's for your Holy Spirit to handle and what's for your soul to endure. The reason why I use the word endure instead of handle for your soul is because your Holy Spirit comes straight from God. Like I said, it's your strength. Yet the soul endures because it takes on some complex emotions.

R. E. P. E. A. T.
resolve. edify. pursue. evolve. amplify. teach.

The Important Trio
Teach

Keeping them from physically damaging your body. Your soul endures them to keep them from weakening your Spirit. Have you ever just gotten really mad or lost someone, and it just tore you up? Have you heard of people who passed away because their emotions were too much to bear after they lost someone close? That rage that you may have felt that made you have super strength; that hurt you felt hurt so bad that you had to fall to your knees? You thought you'd never recover, yet you did somehow; that's your soul. The reason you don't just instantly die is because your soul is strong enough to endure most of the intense emotions that you may have felt. All the things that have happened within the years of your life that your Spirit guided you through were, in turn, strengthening your soul. So when that tough emotional task came by this time, your soul was strong enough to endure it all. See, that's why they work hand in hand to either get you past it or not, depending on the strength. The reason why your soul is strong enough to endure most things is because, in the times that you were going through, you knew enough to call on the strength of your Holy Spirit to help guide you.

R. E. P. E. A. T.
resolve. edify. pursue. evolve. amplify. teach.

This makes you stronger, so your soul didn't have to take all the weight of whatever it was that was challenging or testing you. So, as you can see, if you don't know how to utilize the Holy Spirit that God has given you as a safety guide when you do get to that hard emotion, your soul is not equipped, nor is it strong enough to endure it alone. You just falter.

Your last of this order in the trio can start to feel the deep burden of your soul; you can get sick or even die. It's a harsh reality, but your body can not withstand these hard emotions. It was never designed to be in its delicacy. The Holy Spirit and your soul were put to be in that particular order to keep your physical body from that. God knows what we can handle. That's why he meant for your life to be lived in this order so that you can be in alignment if you haven't realized lol. The physical body is complex and brilliantly made. It's delicate where it needs to be, yet it can also be physically strong. If you work out your body, you'll have physical strength, but it's still delicate.

R. E. P. E. A. T.
resolve. edify. pursue. evolve. amplify. teach.

The Important Trio
Teach

With all that physical strength, you can still catch a cold or get a paper cut. That physical strength from working out just made you physically strong; it did nothing for your emotions or your Spirit. Working out was meant to keep your body healthy enough to endure physical things that come to attack your body. Even still, God makes our bodies so uniquely complex that there is always something in us to try to fight, whatever sickness may be. God knows how important it is to be healthy, and that's why he doesn't want us to be lazy when my Spirit told me to put my task list in this book. I was like, why? My Spirit was like this: God wants us not to be lazy, and now that you have help, it's time to be of help. Even though we have a day of rest there's work to be done to have something to rest from. Work is important for quality of life, and so is rest. God knew what resting does for your body. Every time you sleep, your body is hard at work doing just what God has told it to. Your brain usually tells your body what to do, but when it's in its comatose sleep state, it's doing just what God designed it to do without your brain telling it to.

R. E. P. E. A. T.

resolve. edify. pursue. evolve. amplify. teach.

It's healing you, so that paper cut that your strong self got is healing, lol that cold that your strong self caught it's killing it with rest. That's why it's important: not too much and not too little. Your physical body was also not meant to handle the weight of an emotional meltdown, so if you keep that balance, all things will work together. When you do get weak, you know who to lean on, so you'll never have to put that heavy weight on your body that it can't hold. It's not a physical weight. Therefore, your body doesn't have the strength for it; it just wasn't designed to. That's why keeping that balance of alignment in that order is so, so, important. They work hand in hand. Hopefully, now you can tell that if you were to put one before the other, like your body first, it wouldn't be possible to handle it. Let these things that God has set forth in us help us. God put them there for this very reason. They can't just sit there, though. They have to be used to have that strength to guide, endure, and help you through when you need them. So use them, and make life somewhat easier on yourself.

R. E. P. E. A. T.
resolve. edify. pursue. evolve. amplify. teach.

The Important Trio
Teach

If you're going through this, ask God to help you, and ask God to align you: Spirit, soul, and body. Then, don't fret; be ready for the realignment. When God starts to allow things in your life, just know it's to strengthen you, each part of you. So be ready with the tools that he's given us to help us through. Sometimes, it's going to hurt, but lean on your Holy Spirit to guide you through, and everything else, as long as you keep yourself in alignment, will fall into place. After you've been adjusted, God will be there to keep working those muscles to keep you stronger and bring you back to that perfect peace. That peace surpasses all understanding. God.

R. E. P. E. A. T.
resolve. edify. pursue. evolve. amplify. teach.

Chapter 11
Move Slow

R. E. P. E. A. T.
resolve. edify. pursue. evolve. amplify. teach.

Move Slow
Teach

God says to be slow to anger, to speak, and quick to listen because when we are in a state of anger or rage, we make wrong choices. It's hard to hear our Spirit guide us away from things when upset because anger fills all the gaps. Let's be clear just as God is clear. We are all sinners saved by grace. There is no perfect person. However, God says to repent consistently. Jesus says to deny yourself for him and to daily pick up your cross, to go and sin no more. So, if you think that you can continue to sin, committing the same sin over and over, this is false. It's when you are growing and have learned from that sin that you're a child of God, and he forgives you. Our Father is a God of order, and everything God has created progresses through time, age, our bodies, the waters, and trees. They start at one point and continue to grow bigger and stronger. Because we are children made by God, It is only perfected and prophetic that we continue to grow and progress. When we do sin, remember that we are all sinners saved by grace. If we're not progressing from that sin and learning from it, we are still a sinner.

God will not be pleased with us; neither will his grace be upon us. Only when we fall completely back into God's grace will we proceed in his grace. Being the person I'm meant to be is making me more mature in my daily life, by fault or design. For example. It doesn't bother me if someone pulls out in front of me because they think they have enough time to or they have enough room. Looking at our lives, we don't always make the best choices clearly. So, I no longer get mad at trivial things like that because now I understand it. You can tell how selfish people are just by driving. If you're on a two-lane road and you're going slower than others, instead of getting over or letting a person pass when you see them speeding and choosing to get a ticket or not. Some people break in front of them, and some people purposely just sit there and go slow. You never know what's going on with someone else; who knows why they're speeding? Someone could be on their way to a hospital or their child. It could be someone about to pass away they want to say goodbye to; we never know.

Also, people will gawk to see when there's an accident on the side of the road, slowing down to see what happened, even to be nosey. What does looking at them sadden or upset do for anyone, and how does it help the person in dismay? I know some people will read that and say it's proper to slow down, but I rarely see people doing just that. It's like watching a fight at school and just standing by to see the action. You can tell just by driving how much people assume and are childishly selfish. We must do better in these little things, not just the big things that are important to us. We should immediately pray for people going through things in whatever capacity because we never know. They may have totaled their only vehicle and are now trying to figure out how to get to work. This may cause them to lose their job, or it could be the worst fate that someone has lost their life. We don't know because it didn't happen to us. To not offer some type of help, even with a quick prayer, should never be. Here's another example of something I witnessed that makes me less selfish and slow to anger when I drive.

R. E. P. E. A. T.
resolve. edify. pursue. evolve. amplify. teach.

I remember driving once years ago, and this woman in front of me was driving super slow. We were on a one-lane road, and I was in a hurry, running late for something. When I finally got to go around this woman, I was so upset. You know, when you drive around someone that you feel is irritating you or annoying you, what's the first thing you're going to do? Look at them; you might say something to them, or you might just look at them. In your head, you might've been saying the entire time that you had to deal with this person, "I know this is a." You know, whatever type of person gets on your nerves. The whole time, assuming why they were going slow, assuming that it was a male or a female or someone of a particular race. Well, when I got around this woman, I looked at her, ready to just go off because she was holding me up. My entitled self. She was holding me up from something that I cannot even remember to this day; that is just how trivial it was. The look on her face was something that I will never forget. This woman had a look of fear, pain, and hurt on her face as I passed by her.

R. E. P. E. A. T.
resolve. edify. pursue. evolve. amplify. teach.

Move Slow
Teach

This woman's face was soaked from so many tears that she was crying. At that moment, the fact that she was a woman, what her race was, nothing that I was going on in my head about mattered or compared to that look. I felt horrible that day, and since that day, I have realized that you never know what someone is going through. It's not ok to selfishly assume that everyone is trying to do something to us purposely all the time. I knew at that moment that wherever I was trying to get to, me being late for it was nothing compared to the pain and suffering this person was feeling. Because I am human and have a conscience, my Spirit is relevant in my life, so I empathized with what that woman was going through. I should've asked her if she was OK or offered to pray for her, but because of my embarrassment and childishness, I just kept driving. Who knows, whatever happened to that woman, she could've been suicidal, she could've been in need, and I could've helped. Looking back, this was so selfish of me, and if given that opportunity to help her now, regardless of anything else, I would.

R. E. P. E. A. T.
resolve. edify. pursue. evolve. amplify. teach.

These days, when I'm behind someone and they're going slow, they're swerving, or speeding behind me, I empathize with that person; I move and let them pass. I ask them if they're ok if they are swerving or going slow in front of me because I'm more patient. God says that when you are a child, you do as a child and think as a child. Yet, when you become a woman or a man, you do as a man and think as a man or a woman. So, in hindsight, when you become grown, you're supposed to mature. There is supposed to be a progression from when we were a child. As adults or teens who can drive also, we should never feel more entitled than the next. It could very well be that any of us in this same position one day need help. For all of us adults behaving like children. Let's fix what needs to be fixed in the small things of our lives so that we can be mature and in progress as we move forward by God's grace.

Chapter 12
Words From The Wise

R. E. P. E. A. T.
resolve. edify. pursue. evolve. amplify. teach.

That saying, Father knows best, is a true and understated understatement. How many of us are wise enough to listen to the wise people of age and their experiences around us? Why do you think older people take their time to speak when asked a question? They pause to go through all their wisdom to give you the best truthful answer. They've made mistakes and want to give you the best answer. A wise man won't just blurt out the first thing that comes to mind because he wants to answer in wisdom and truth, not just with his mind. This elder may see that you're headed down the wrong path and wants to give you the best answer so that he won't make any more mistakes. If I'm going up to a door and I see that someone's just coming from it, and I go all the way up to it just to find out it's closed. The first thing I'm going to think is, when you walked right past me, why couldn't you warn me before I walked all the way there that it was closed? That person could have saved me a trip, right? Why are we ok with wasting a trip, time, or money?

R. E. P. E. A. T.
resolve. edify. pursue. evolve. amplify. teach.

Words From The Wise
Repeat

This wise person may not have it all together or figured out, but they're telling you about something that they know and have figured out. One thing I know about elders is they don't hold their tongue from the truth, and they don't have any reason to lie about something that only benefits you. They've been there before. They went down that very road, and it was horrible, so they took time to stop and tell you before you wasted your time, money, emotions, etc. That, hey, it's a dead end; it's not worth the trip. Is it silly for us not to listen? To just waste time and effort or whatever else to just see for ourselves? Why would someone take that time to steer you wrong? Especially if it's something that will positively affect your life. So, you went to the door anyway to see if it was really closed, a dead end, and what do you know to your surprise? It was. Wow, imagine that. You spent that time and effort to see for yourself, and what did it change? Did it make you wiser to go through it and see for yourself than it did to just hear and believe it from someone who had already been?

R. E. P. E. A. T.
resolve. edify. pursue. evolve. amplify. teach.

Did it change the truth that was already told to you? Or did you just waste time when you're not promised tomorrow? Does the devil really have any new tricks when I can comb through the Bible and find stories and passages that are relevant in this current time? Think. The devil is quite clever in getting you to think that you're accomplishing something by being independent and not listening to wisdom. If he can get you to see the areas where this person is weak, where they don't have it all together. Where even in their old age, an experience they hadn't barked upon. Just to waste your time in hopes that you don't make it in time to see the truth. So, your pride and judgment aid you in wasting precious time. These are things that the devil plays on. You have to be strong in who you are. Maybe they've gone to that door 30 times over before you even got this wisdom. Maybe the other pathway or door around the corner they're still stuck on. So you don't see a reason to listen because now they're a hypocrite. If it's coming from a place of love, then where's it coming from? Think.

They may have stumbled in life or been stuck in some places, but there has been grace and mercy in their life to be here still. Instead of using common sense, having less pride, and simply listening to understand, we wrongly judge and miss it. We miss what God is saying through wisdom. So now I come to this. People say that the Bible is fake. It was written to just keep you in line to control you, to make you submissive. The people who helped write it were probably Hippocrates or didn't have it all together. They're just stories that some doped-up men wrote and were created like a regular novel. Well, let me say this. Firstly, I would implore you to study how difficult it would have to be for someone to tamper with or rewrite the Bible. In addition, can someone show me in the Bible where there is something that's being said that doesn't have to do with love? That doesn't have to do with propelling your life to help you in any way. Giving you wisdom and knowledge from people who have been down this all too familiar road?

What I see are wise people who have experience and wisdom from the mistakes that they've made. That has gone the wrong way or done the wrong thing, and that is now trying to save us that trip. Who knows now, but God, how many times did they have to go down that road to gain their wisdom? I listen and read now to understand, so I know that the elders of today are in many ways the same as the elders from then. They weren't very different. They may have had different lingo or clothes that they wore. The needs may have been different, but God has remained the same. The devil has been doing the same kill, steal, and destroy routine in hopes that you lack the knowledge to listen to wisdom, so why not listen? They've been here, done this, and helped write the book! Literally! Why not save time? Why not listen? I was talking to someone the other day about a famous athlete. They were telling me what they thought about an incident that he was in by reading what they saw on the internet. I gave my opinion on it, and of course, we disagreed. What could we say, though, but what is our opinion?

Unless we sat down with the pair of people who were involved, how would we know? We didn't have all the pieces to the puzzle to make a true judgment. Even then, if we all sat down, who would say the truth would still come out? Someone wise who had gone through to make such a true statement that there are three sides to every story: one side, the other side, and the truth. It makes sense. Since we've not lived in that time or been able to meet Jesus or see if these stories in the Bible ever happened, how can we say they're not true? How can we make a true judgment? We can't. I know that when we grow a relationship with God, we gain the truth, and our Holy Spirit confirms it. I know that when you take the time to read the Bible, something that you are going through that you're having a problem with, it's no coincidence that the people from that day went through it. They wrote about everything and gave you wisdom and direction from the experiences that they've been through because God wanted to give you an easier path.

R. E. P. E. A. T.
resolve. edify. pursue. evolve. amplify. teach.

There's no lie in those things, so why not listen? What are they saying wrong? How would it hurt you? God gave our elders wisdom to form a written book of knowledge and truth, with the addition of a walking visible piece of him to whom he also allowed to die for our sins! There is no excuse. Why should we doubt? It seems to me like the devil is trying to get you to waste time- precious time! Don't waste any more time so that you don't miss something that can take you to the next level of whatever goals that God has burdened you to accomplish. Simply listening to this wisdom might save you some headache, heartache, or frustration. Who knows how much time you have left to waste? You may want to use it wisely in a way that will improve your journey.

R. E. P. E. A. T.
resolve. edify. pursue. evolve. amplify. teach.

Chapter 13
Truth Behind The Journey

R. E. P. E. A. T.
resolve. edify. pursue. evolve. amplify. teach.

When you start to go towards God, be prepared to deal with people not being on your side. Some of those friends that you felt so much for and gave so much energy to may not reciprocate the energy you have now. Darkness runs from the light for fear of what it may lose. The devil will use people to tell you things that may sound like God, but it's not of God, so remember how to know what's God and what's not. To keep you exactly where he'd like you to be, he'll use anyone who is willing. Let me give you an example. When you give your life to God, it's not a quick process. Your soul and body don't just magically change. That's why Paul says we have to die to ourselves daily because you're still you, but hopefully with a new lens. Slowly changing day by day sometimes and moment by moment. Don't get me wrong; God says that when you give your life fully over to him, you are born again.

R. E. P. E. A. T.
resolve. edify. pursue. evolve. amplify. teach.

It's your journey in this world that tries to keep you in the darkness that we have to fight away constantly. We must embrace it for what it is. People will try and tell you that you're playing God or mock you like they did Jesus. Just because you went to a couple of services, do you think you're holier than God now? You're a Christian, but you just had road rage! What type of Christian still does this and that? Don't try and tell me anything; you're fake! Is it not funny how most people say the same things? Or when something big happens with a pastor, they are sure to point it out to you. The enemy uses these things as a detour to keep the narrative in their favor. You're now on a narrow road that is less traveled, so be prepared to see more of the opposite of what God is. Don't let people make you feel like you are no longer a child of God because you may have a bad moment.

People will make your mind run if you forget what God says or whom you've become in the Lord; don't do that to yourself. If you internalize it, then you start to doubt and feel bad about your choices. You may start to think you're a fake, a hypocrite, no longer worthy of the love of God; know where it's coming from; it's not God. When we pass away, there's a reason why our bodies stay here, but they are no longer usable. Your Spirit and soul are gone. It was the breath of life you needed, which was highly important for you to function in your body. Without it, your physical body becomes lifeless. So, what do you think you're really fighting against? Their Spirit, or the Spirits around them. It's not the flesh that we pound on when we get upset by fighting flesh against flesh. It's the devil or one of his minions using them to try and keep you from your destined self.

It's going to take time and effort to get stronger, but now you're on the right track. As long as you put forth the right things with God first, God will be for you, and no man that God has created could go against it. It's you just choosing to be more in the Holy Spirit, which creates a healthy relationship with God. There's a season of repair going on; it takes time, love, and patience; it takes you doing, giving, and having some things we touched on before. Patience to learn, teach, and be taught. The kindness of others and yourself for those that you know and don't know. Forgiveness, for yourself and others who were just as lost and manipulated in this world, who were easily tricked by the devil to have a hand in your unforgiveness. These are just some of the things that have been defined as love. Love isn't always pretty; some work comes with love that can be painful for some.

Still, love is the most important thing we need, good or bad. Like you read about before. The more love you seek from God, the more you'll have to give. We need to not use our energy towards the wrong things that keep our minds away from that journey. This is a harder task to do than just living life carelessly. It's easier to circle the things that you can physically see and touch. It takes strength in the truth to continue to see God all around us with the eyes of the Holy Spirit. There's a reason why it says in the Bible that this is a road less traveled; it's harder, yet more rewarding. I know people may say well, I don't live my life carelessly; I'm always on top of my game. Well, here's some real truth. What good is it to gain the world but lose your soul? What good is it to clean your car from top to bottom but not pay the note? Be honest with yourself; I had to. So you know I'm going to tell you the truth!

What good is it to take care of all you do in this world and leave out the creator of it? What good is it to do all that exercise and leave out the one who breathed you life? That's like being mean to the Mother who gave birth to you; it just makes no sense. That's the one woman you should have the utmost respect for. We should have the utmost respect for the father of all creation! I'm just saying. When you have that! You'll have love; you'll give love and receive it. You'll start to understand that love is beautiful from all corners of life, from all races of people. Nonetheless, first things first, you have to give more of yourself. Are the things and the people that you've grown inseparable from are they on this same path? Would you give your life if it came to it or keep them? Would you still choose God if you had to choose between the two?

R. E. P. E. A. T.

resolve. edify. pursue. evolve. amplify. teach.

Maybe you'd give your life for them because you love them so, but would you give your child's life just to keep them? So, maybe you don't have any kids, would you give your career or your money? Basically, what are the things that you cherish the most? Would you give them to supplement your life to be with God? Well, if you've asked God to be your Lord and Savior, then you're doing that! I had to make it up in my Spirit, soul, and body that I was worth all of what God has for me now and for his future. I can't continue to give myself to my will and not God's, the things that will not bring me closer to God and his authority. I'm not putting all of what I have in God on the line for a lie that can be taken from me at any moment. Let us all be strong and show strength in God no matter how heavy the load is because God will not leave us to journey alone.

R. E. P. E. A. T.
resolve. edify. pursue. evolve. amplify. teach.

Final
Words

R. E. P. E. A. T.

resolve. edify. pursue. evolve. amplify. teach.

You have done it!!!! You have reached the end. You could, and you did! I, for one, am proud of you. So how do you feel? Hopefully, accomplished. Since you have made it to the end now, you should understand why it was so important for you to write those things out with pure, unadulterated remembrance without unconsciously leaving things out. Now is the time you take your paper and read it. Since the beginning of our lives, so much has happened that we've forgotten about it. We have become complacent, blocked out hurtful things, or forgotten about them. No matter what you have written on your paper about you, no matter what it is, let this be a reference to something that you can always look back on to remind you not just of your beginning but to give you a better understanding of the person you are.

R. E. P. E. A. T.
resolve. edify. pursue. evolve. amplify. teach.

Like why you may get angry, why you may not feel loved, where this loneliness comes from, or why you can not see love even if it's given to you. It is a reference to constantly look upon, propel you forward, and help you to see how far you have come. In moments of self-reflection something that you can look back at and say that is why I am that way. This is why I have the issue. What is the saying if you know better, you do better? Well, now that you know, do. Get better with things in your life so that you can now teach. Teach the ones around you also how to do better, lend them your book to start them on a better pathway. Lastly, it's time to receive when you have gotten a rhythm of self-forgiveness or forgiveness for others who have harmed you, and your heart is open to love.

R. E. P. E. A. T.
resolve. edify. pursue. evolve. amplify. teach.

Receive the only real peace that you will ever find on this earth. Yes, the love and peace of your father. Our creator, Lord God almighty! The perfect ending for us all! Read the Bible. Start from the beginning to have a complete understanding of the beginning and why we are so loved and important to God. My prayer for you love, is that you are filled and that your cup is overflowing. Your compass is now set in the right direction, and you will receive the ultimate love from the ultimate sacrifice for your life. In addition, I pray that you meet teachers everywhere you go who propel you even further down the correct path. I pray you are constantly filled with love and have nothing but love to give.

R. E. P. E. A. T.

resolve. edify. pursue. evolve. amplify. teach.

I pray that whenever you feel alone, you remember that you are never alone, and God sends the perfect company your way to fill you with joy and the presence of God. I pray that you continue to move forward and never backward from things that have held you back and that you have now been healed. My prayer is that everyone who touches and reads this book let it be a blessing to you and amplify you in the way it was intended. I love you.
Amen. Shalom

R. E. P. E. A. T.

resolve. edify. pursue. evolve. amplify. teach.

Contents

To Follow The Correct Path,
You Must Start At The
Beginning

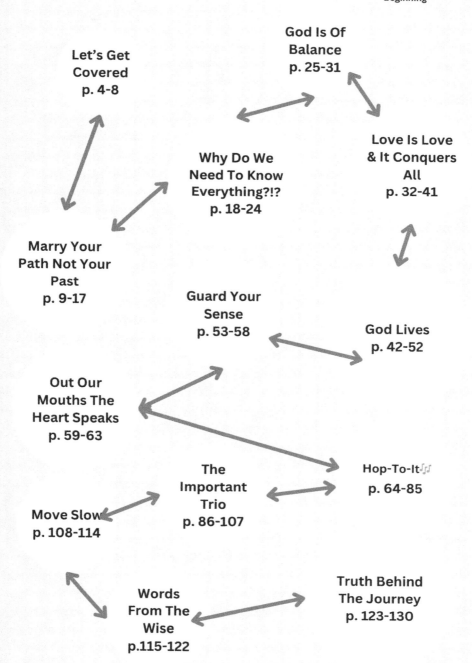

R. E. P. E. A. T.
resolve. edify. pursue. evolve. amplify. teach.

I am just giving thanks to God and my family for their patience, love, and understanding.

Made in the USA
Monee, IL
15 September 2024

65319365R00079